Scillaes Metamorphosis by Thomas Lodge

Enterlaced with The Unfortunate Love of Glaucus

As can be easily understood presenting an exact chronicle of the facts in the life of a 16th Century playwright is often difficult. Thomas Lodge is no exception.

Thomas Lodge, born around 1558 in west Ham, was the second son of Sir Thomas Lodge, the Lord Mayor of London, and his third wife Anne.

Lodge was educated at Merchant Taylors' School and thence to Trinity College, Oxford; taking his BA in 1577 and his MA in 1581.

Lodge, disregarded his parents career wishes in order to take up literature. When the penitent Stephen Gosson published his Schoole of Abuse in 1579, Lodge responded with Defence of Poetry, Music and Stage Plays (1579 or 1580). His pamphlet was banned, but appears to have been circulated privately.

Already in 1580 Lodge had published a volume of poems entitled Scillaes Metamorphosis, Enterlaced with the Unfortunate Love of Glaucus, also more briefly known as Glaucus and Scilla.

Lodge seems to have married his first wife Joan in or shortly before 1583, when, "impressed with the uncertainty of human life", he made a will. That his family viewed his conduct at the time with disdain may be noted by the absence of his name from his father's will in 1583.

The marriage of Lodge and Joan produced a daughter, Mary. However, without an income from his family Lodge would have to provide it by other means.

The debate in pamphlets between Lodge and Gosson continued with Gosson's Playes Confuted in Five Actions; and Lodge retorting with his Alarum Against Usurers (1585)—a "tract for the times".

That same year, 1585, he produced his first tale written in prose and verse, The Delectable History of Forbonius and Prisceria.

Lodge appears to have been at sea on a number of long voyages. Usually these are described as 'freebooting voyages', an interchangeable term also used for piracy and plunder. Many nations endorsed these tactics and it seems fairly safe to suggest that these voyages were a source of revenue which would keep Joan and Mary with their heads above water. These long voyages also provided something else that Lodge would have been keen to gather and usefully use; time. During the expedition to Terceira and the Canaries (around 1586), to set aside the tedium of his voyage, Lodge composed his prose tale of Rosalynde, Euphues Golden Legacie, which, printed in 1590, would later be used by Shakespeare as the basis for As You Like It.

Before starting on his next voyage, this time to South America, Lodge published a historical romance, The History of Robert, Second Duke of Normandy, surnamed Robert the Devil; and he left behind him for publication Catharos Diogenes in his Singularity, a discourse on the immorality of Athens (London). Both appeared in 1591.

By now Lodge was on a voyage with Thomas Cavendish to Brazil and the Straits of Magellan and would only be able to return home in 1593. Whilst he was travelling another romance in the manner of Lyly, Euphues Shadow, the Battaile of the Sences, appeared in 1592.

At either end of this voyage Lodge appears to have worked on some dramas, most notably with Robert Greene.

It is thought that in 1590, together with Greene, he wrote A Looking Glass for London and England (published 1594). He had already written The Wounds of Civil War (produced perhaps as early as 1587, and published in 1594, and put on as a play reading at the Globe Theatre on 7 February 1606), a good second-rate piece in the half-chronicle fashion of its age.

His second historical romance, the Life and Death of William Longbeard (1593), was more successful than the first. Lodge also brought back with him from the new world voyage A Margarite of America (published 1596), a romance between a Peruvian prince and a daughter of the king of Muscovy interspersed with many lyrics.

The composition of Phillis, a volume and an early sonnet cycle sequence (an increasingly popular format in Elizabethan times), was published with the narrative poem, The Complaynte of Elsired, in 1593.

A Fig for Momus was published in 1595 and gained him the accolade of being the earliest English satirist. This work contains eclogues addressed to Daniel and others as well as an epistle addressed to Michael Drayton.

In the latter part of his life—possibly about 1596, when he published his Wits Miserie and the World's Madnesse, which is dated from Low Leyton in Essex, and the religious tract Prosopopeia (if, as seems probable, it was his), in which he repents of his "lewd lines" of other days—he became a Catholic and engaged in the practice of medicine, for which Wood says he qualified himself by a degree at Avignon, in France, in 1600. Two years later he received the degree of M.D. from Oxford University.

Early in 1606 he seems to have left England, to escape the persecution then directed against the Catholics; and a letter from him dated 1610 thanks the English ambassador in Paris for enabling him to return in safety.

At some point in his later life Lodge appears to have married again. This time to Jane Aldred, the widow of Solomon Aldred, at one time a Roman Catholic agent of Francis Walsingham in Rome.

From the early 1600's Lodge appears to have written or published sparingly. His later works include A Treatise of the Plague (1603) and two major translations—The Famous and Memorable Works of Josephus (1602) and The Works of Lucius Annaeus Seneca (1614), both of these went through several editions.

Obviously with his conversion to the Catholic faith life would have been difficult and most accounts agree that he withdrew from a literary life and instead concentrated on his work as a doctor. Over the years he was increasingly recognized as a distinguished physician and finally worked from Old Fish Street in the parish of St. Mary Magdalen.

Thomas Lodge died in London, most probably during an outbreak of the plague, in 1625.

Index of Contents

I

Walking alone (all onely full of griefe)
Within a thicket nere to Isis floud,
Weeping my wants, and wailing scant reliefe,
Wringing mine armes (as one with sorrowe wood);
The piteous streames relenting at my mone
Withdrew their tides, and staid to heare me grone.

II

From foorth the channell, with a sorrowing crie
The Sea-god Glaucus (with his hallowed heares
Wet in the teares of his sad mothers dye)
With piteous lookes before my face appeares;
For whome the Nimphes a mossie coate did frame.
Embroadered with his Sillas heavenly name.

III

And as I sat under a Willow tree,
The lovelie honour of faire Thetis bower
Reposd his head upon my faintfull knee:
And when my teares had ceast their stormie shower
He dried my cheekes, and then bespake him so,
As when he waild I straight forgot my woe:

IV

Infortunate, why wandreth thy content
From forth his scope as wearied of it selfe?
Thy bookes have schoold thee from this fond repent,
And thou canst talke by proofe of wavering pelfe:
Unto the world such is inconstancie,

As sapp to tree, as apple to the eye.

V

Marke, how the morne in roseat colour shines,
And straight with cloudes the Sunnie tract is clad;
Then see how pomp through waxe and waine declines,
From high to lowe, from better to the bad:
Take moist from Sea, take colour from his kinde,
Before the world devoid of change thou finde.

VI

With secret eye looke on the earth a while,
Regard the changes Nature forceth there;
Behold the heavens, whose course all sence beguile;
Respect thy selfe, and thou shalt find it cleere,
That infantlike thou art become a youth,
And youth forespent a wretched age ensu'th.

VII

In searching then the schoolemens cunning noates,
Of heaven, of earth, of flowers, of springing trees,
Of hearbs, of mettall, and of Thetis floates,
Of lawes and nurture kept among the Bees:
Conclude and knowe times change by course of fate,
Then mourne no more, but moane my haples state.

VIII

Here gan he pause and shake his heavie head,
And fould his armes, and then unfould them straight;
Faine would he speake, but tongue was charm'd by dread,
WhiPst I that sawe what woes did him awaight,
Comparing his mishaps and moane with mine,
Gan smile for joy and drie his drooping eyne.

IX

But (loe) a wonder; from the channels glide
A sweet melodious noyse of musicke rose,
That made the streame to dance a pleasant tide,

The weedes and sallowes neere the bancke that groes
Gan sing, as when the calmest windes accorde
To greete with balmie breath the fleeting forde.

X

Upon the silver bosome of the streame
First gan faire Themis shake her amber locks,
Whom all the Nimphs that waight on Neptunes realme
Attended from the hollo we of the rocks.
In briefe, while these rare parragons assemble,
The watrie world to touch their teates doo tremble.

XI

Footing it featlie on the grassie ground,
These Damsels circling with their brightsome faires
The love-sicke God and I, about us wound
Like starres that Ariadnes crowne repaires:
Who once hath seene or pride of morne, or day,
Would deeme all pompe within their cheekes did play.

XII

Nais faire Nimph with Bacchus ivorie touch,
Gan tune a passion with such sweete reports,
And everie word, noate, sigh, and pause was such,
And everie Cadence fed with such consorts,
As were the Delian Harper bent to heare,
Her statelie straines might tempt his curious eare.

XIII

Of love (God wot) the lovelie Nimph complained:
But so of love as forced Love to love her;
And even in love such furious love remained,
As searching out his powrefull shaft to prove her,
He found his quiver emptied of the best,
And felt the arrowe sticking in his breast.

XIV

Under a Popler Themis did repose her,

And from a brier a sweetfull branch did plucke:
When midst the brier ere she could scarce suppose her
A Nightingale gan sing: but woe the lucke;
The branch so neere her breast, while she did quicke her
To turne her head, on sodaine gan to pricke her.

XV

WhiPst smiling Clore midst her envious blushes,
Gan blame her feare and pretilie said thus;
Worse prickes than these are found among these bushes,
And yet such prickes are scarcelie feard of us.
Nay soft (said Chelis), prickes doo make birds sing,
But prickes in Ladies bosomes often sting.

XVI

Thus jest they on the Nightingales report,
And on the prickle of the Eglantine,
On Nais song, and all the whole consort
In publique this sweete sentence did assigne;
That while some smile; some sigh through change of time;
Some smart, some sport amidst their youthlie prime.

XVII

Such wreathes as bound the Thebans ivorie brow;
Such gay trickt garlands pleit these jollie Dames;
The flowres themselves when as the Nimphes gan vowe,
Gan vaile their crestes in honour of their names:
And smilde their sweete and woed with so much glee,
As if they said, sweet Nimph, come gather mee.

XVIII

But pencive Glaucus, passionate with painings,
Amidst their revell thus began his ruth;
Nimphes, flie these Groves late blasted with my plainings,
For cruell Silla nill regard my truth:
And leave us two consorted in our gronings,
To register with teares our bitter monings.

XIX

The flouds doo faile their course to see our crosse,
The fields forsake their greene to heare our griefe,
The rockes will weepe whole springs to marke our losse,
The hills relent to store our scant reliefe,
The aire repines, the pencive birds are heavie,
The trees to see us paind no more are lea vie.

XX

Ay me, the Shepheards let their flockes want feeding,
And flockes to see their palie face are sorie,
The Nimphes to spie the flockes and shepheards needing
Prepare their teares to heare our tragicke storie:
Whilst we surprisde with griefe cannot disclose them,
With sighing wish the world for to suppose them.

XXI

He that hath seene the sweete Arcadian boy
Wiping the purple from his forced wound,
His pretie teares betokening his annoy,
His sighes, his cries, his falling on the ground,
The Ecchoes ringing from the rockes his fall,
The trees with teares reporting of his thrall:

XXII

And Venus starting at her love-mates crie,
Forcing hir birds to hast her chariot on;
And full of griefe at last with piteous eie
Seene where all pale with death he lay alone,
Whose beautie quaild, as wont the Lillies droop
When wastfull winter windes doo make them stoop:

XXIII

Her daintie hand addrest to dawe her deere,
Her roseall lip alied to his pale cheeke,
Her sighes, and then her lookes and heavie cheere,
Her bitter threates, and then her passions meeke;
How on his senseles corpes she lay a crying,
As if the boy were then but new a dying.

XXIV

He that hath vewd Angelica the faire
Bestraught with fancie nere the Caspian springs:
Renting the tresses of her golden haire,
How on her harpe with pitious notes she sings
Of Rolands ruth, of Medors false depart,
Sighing each rest from center of her heart.

XXV

How now she writes upon a beechen bow
Her Medors name, and bedlam like againe
Calls all the heaven to witnes of his vow,
And straight againe begins a mournefull straine,
And how in thought of her true faith forsooken
He fled her bowres, and how his league was broken.

XXVI

Aye me who markes her harpe hang up againe
Upon the willowes watered with her teares,
And how she rues to read her Rolands paine,
When but the shadowe of his name appeares;
Would make more plainings from his eyes to flee
Than teares distill from amber weeping tree.

XXVII

He that hath knowne the passionate mishappes
That nere Olimpus faire Lucina felt
When as her Latium love her fancie trappes,
How with suspect her inward soule dooth melt:
Or markt the Morne her Cephalus complaining,
May then recount the course of all our paining.

XXVIII

But tender Nimphes, to you belongs no teene;
Then favor me in flying from this bower
Whereas but care and thought of crosses been,
Leave me that loose my selfe through fancies power,
Through fancies power which had I leave to loose it,

No fancie then should see me for to choose it.

XXIX

When you are fled, the Heaven shall lowre for sorrowe,
The day orecast shalbe bedtime with sable,
The aire from Sea such streaming showres shall borrow
As earth to beare the brunt shall not be able,
And shippes shall safely saile whereas beforne
The ploughman watcht the reaping of his corne.

XXX

Goe you in peace to Neptunes watrie sound,
No more may Glaucus play him with so prettie;
But shun resort where solace nill be found,
And plaine my Scillaes pride and want of pittie:
Alas sweet Nimphs, my Godhead's all in vaine,
For why this brest includes immortall paine.

XXXI

Scilla hath eyes, but too sweete eyes hath Scilla;
Scilla hath hands, faire hands but coy in touching;
Scilla in wit surpasseth grave Sibilla,
Scilla hath words, but words well storde with grutching;
Scilla a Saint in looke, no Saint in scorning:
Looke Saint-like Scilla, least I die with mourning.

XXXII

Alas why talke I? Sea-god, cease to mourne her,
For in her nay my joyes are ever ceasing:
Cease life or love, then shall I never blame her;
But neither love nor life may finde decreasing.
A mortall wound is my immortall being,
Which passeth thought, or eyes advised seeing.

XXXIII

Herewith his faltring tongue by sighs oppressed
Forsooke his office, and his bloud resorted
To feede the heart that wholly was distressed,

Whilst pale (like Pallas flowre) my knee supported
His feeble head and arme, so full of anguish,
That they which sawe his sorrowes gan to languish.

XXXIV

Themis the coyest of this beauteous traine
On hillie toppes the wonderous Moly found.
Which dipt in balmie deaw she gan to straine,
And brought her present to recure his wound:
Clore she gathered Amaranthus flower,
And Nais Ajax blossom in that stowre.

XXXV

Some chafe his temples with their lovelie hands,
Some sprinkle water on his pale wan cheekes,
Some weepe, some wake, some curse affections bandes;
To see so young, so faire, become so weake:
But not their pitious hearbs, or springs have working,
To ease that heart where wanton love is lurking.

XXXVI

Naithles, though loath to shewe his holy kindnes,
On everie one he spent a looke for favour,
And prayed their pardon, vouching Cupids blindnes,
(Oh fancies fond that naught but sorrowes savour);
To see a lovely God leave Sea Nimphes so:
Who cannot doome upon his deadly woe?

XXXVII

Themis that knewe that waters long restrained
Breake foorth with greater billowes than the brookes
That swetely float through meades with flowres distained,
With cheerefull laies did raise his heavie lookes;
And bad him speake and tell what him agreev'd:
For griefes disclos'd (said she) are soone releev'd.

XXXVIII

And as she wisht, so all the rest did woe him;

By whose incessant suites at last invited,
He thus discovered that which did undoo him,
And orderlie his hideous harmes recited,
When first which fingers wagge he gan to still them,
And thus with drierie tearmes of love did fill them.

XXXIX

Ah Nimphes (quoth he), had I by reason learnt
That secret art which birdes have gaind by sence,
By due foresight misfortune to prevent;
Or could my wit controule mine eyes offence:
You then should smile and I should tell such stories,
As woods, and waves should triumph in our glories.

XL

But Nereus daughters, Sea-borne Saints attend,
Lake-breeding Geese when from the Easterne clime
They list unto the westerne waters wend
To choose their place of rest by course of time,
Approaching Taurus haughtie topped hill
They charme their cackle by this wondrous skill.

XLI

The climing mountaine neighbouring ayre welnie,
Hath harbored in his rockes and desart haunts
Whole airies of Eagles, prest to flie
That gazing on the Sonne their birth right vaunts,
Which birds of Jove with deadlie fewde pursue
The wandering Geese, when so they presse in vewe.

XLII

These fearefull flitting troopes by nature tought,
Passing these dangerous places of pursuit:
When all the desart vales they through have sought,
With pibbles stop their beakes to make them mute,
And by this meanes their dangerous deathes prevent
And gaine their wished waters of frequent*.

*frequent, resort

XLIII

But I fond God, (I God complaine thy follie)
Let birds by sense exceede my reason farre:
Whilom than I who was more strong and jollie
Who more contemnd affections wanton warre?
Who lesse than I lov'd lustfull Cupids arrowes?
Who now with curse & plagues poore Glaucus harrowes.

XLIV

How have I leapt to heare the Tritons play
A harsh retreat unto the swelling flouds?
How have I kept the Dolphins at a bay,
When as I ment to charme their wanton moods?
How have the angrie windes growne calme for love,
When as these fingers did my harpe strings move?

XLV

Was any Nimph, you Nimphes, was ever any
That tangled not her fingers in my tresse?
Some well I wot and of that some full many
Wisht or my faire, or their desire were lesse:
Even Ariadne, gazing from the skie
Became enamorde of poore Glaucus eye.

XLVI

Amidst this pride of youth and beauties treasure
It was my chaunce, you floods can tell my chancing,
Fleeting along Sicillian bounds for pleasure,
To spie a Nimph of such a radiant glancing,
As when I lookt, a beame of subtill firing
From eye to heart incenst a deepe desiring.

XLVII

Ah had the vaile of reason clad mine eye,
This foe of freedome had not burnt my heart:
But birds are blest, and most accurst am I
Who must report her glories to my smart,
The Nimph I sawe and lov'de her, all to cruell

Scilla, faire Scilla, my fond fancies juell.

XLVIII

Her haire not trust, but scatterd on her brow,
Surpassing Hiblas honnie for the view,
Or softned golden wires; I know not how
Love with a radiant beautie did pursue
My too judiciall eyes, in darting fire
That kindled straight in me my fond desire.

XLIX

Within these snares first was my heart intrapped,
Till through those golden shrowdes mine eies did see
An yvorie shadowed front, wherein was wrapped
Those pretie bowres where Graces couched be:
Next which her cheekes appeerd like crimson silk,
Or ruddie rose bespred on whitest milk.

L

Twixt which the nose in lovely tenor bends,
(Too traitrous pretie for a Lovers view:)
Next which her lips like violets commends
By true proportion that which dooth insue;
Which when they smile, present unto the eies
The Oceans pride and yvorie paradice.

LI

Her pollisht necke of milke white snowes doth shine,
As when the Moone in Winter night beholdes them:
Her breast of alablaster cleere and fine,
Whereon two rising apples faire unfolds them,
Like Cinthias face when in her full she shineth,
And blushing to her Love-mates bower declineth.

LII

From whence in length her armes doo sweetly spred
Like two rare branchie saples in the Spring,
Yeelding five lovely sprigs from everie head,

Proportioned alike in everie thing;
Which featly sprout in length like springborne frends,
Whose pretie tops with five sweet roses ends.

LIII

But why alas should I that Marble hide
That doth adorne the one and other flanke,
From whence a mount of quickned snow doth glide;
Or els the vale that bounds this milkwhite banke,
Where Venus and her sisters hide the fount,
Whose lovely Nectar dooth all sweetes surmount.

LIV

Confounded with descriptions, I must leave them;
Lovers must thinke, and Poets must report them:
For silly wits may never well conceave them,
Unlesse a speciall grace from heaven consort them.
Aies me, these faires attending Scilla won me:
But now (sweet Nimphes) attend what hath undon me.

LV

The lovely breast where all this beautie rested,
Shrowded within a world of deepe disdaine:
For where I thought my fancie should be feasted
With kinde affect, alas (unto my paine)
When first I woode, the wanton straight was flying,
And gave repulse before we talkt of trying.

LVI

How oft have I (too often have I done so)
In silent night when everie eye was sleeping,
Drawne neere her cave, in hope her love were won so,
Forcing the neighboring waters through my weeping
To wake the windes, who did afflict her dwelling
Whilst I with teares my passion was a telling.

LVII

When midst the Caspian seas the wanton plaid,

I drew whole wreaths of corrall from the rockes:
And in her lap my heavenly presents laid:
But she unkind rewarded me with mockes,
Such are the fruites that spring from Ladies coying,
Who smile at teares, and are intrapt with toying.

LVIII

Tongue might grow wearie to report my wooings,
And heart might burst to thinke of her deniall:
May none be blamde but heaven for all these dooings,
That yeeld no helpes in midst of all my triall.
Heart, tongue, thought, pen nil serve me to repent me,
Disdaine her selfe should strive for to lament me:

LIX

Wretched Love let me die, end my love by my death;
Dead alas still I live, flie my life, fade my love.
Out alas love abides, still I joy vitall breath:
Death in love, love is death, woe is me that doo prove.
Paine and woe, care & grief e every day about me hovers:
Then but death what can quel al the plages of haples lovers?

LX

Aies me my moanings are like water drops
That neede an age to pearce her marble heart,
I sow'd true zeale, yet fruiteles were my crop:
I plighted faith, yet falsehoode wrought my smart:
I praisd her lookes, her lookes dispised Glaucus,
Was ever amorous Sea-god scorned thus?

LXI

A hundereth swelling tides my mother spent
Upon these lockes, and all hir Nimphes were prest,
To pleit them faire when to her bowre I went:
He that hath seene the wandring Phoebus crest,
Toucht with the Christall of Eurotas spring,   •
The pride of these my bushie locks might sing.

LXII

But short discourse beseemes my bad successe,
Eache office of a lover I performed:
So fervently my passions did her presse,
So sweete my laies, my speech so well reformed,
That (cruell) when she sawe naught would begile me,
With angrie lookes the Nimph did thus exile me:

LXIII

Packe hence, thou fondling, to the westerne Seas,
Within some calmy river shrowd thy head:
For never shall my faire thy love appease,
Since fancie from this bosome late is fled:
And if thou love me, shewe it in departing:
For why thy presence dooth procure my smarting,

LXIV

This said with angrie lookes, away she hasted
As fast as flie the flouds before the winds:
When I (poore soule) with wretched sorrowes wasted,
Exclaimde on love, which wit and reason blinds:
And banisht from hir bowre with wofull poasting
I bent my selfe to seeke a forreine coasting.

LXV

At last in wandring through the greater Seas
It was my chance to passe the noted streights:
And wearied sore in seeking after ease,
Amidst the creekes, and watrie coole receits,
I spied from farre by helpe of sonnie beames
A fruitefull He begirt with Ocean streames.

LXVI

Westward I fleeted, and with heedfull eie
Beheld the chalkie cliffes that tempt the aire,
Till at the last it was my chance to spie
A pleasant entrance to the flouds repaire;
Through which I prest, and wondring there beheld
On either side a sweete and fruitfull field.

LXVII

Isis (the Ladie of that lovely streame)
Made holiday in view of my resort;
And all the Nimphes of that her watrie realme
Gan trip for joy, to make me mickle sport:
But I (poore soule) with no such joyes contented,
Forsooke their bowers, and secretly lamented.

LXVIII

All solitarie rome I heere about,
Now on the shoare, now in the streame I weepe,
Fire burnes within, and gastly feare without,
No rest, no ease, no hope of any sleepe:
Poore banisht God, heere have I still remained,
Since time my Scilla hath my sutes disdained.

LXIX

And heere consort I now with haplesse men,
Yeelding them comfort, (though my wound be cureless)
Songs of remorse I warble now and then,
Wherein I curse fond Love and Fortune durelesse,
Wan hope my weale, my trust but bad adventure,
Circumference is care, my heart the center.

LXX

Whilest thus he spake, fierce Ate charmde his tongue,
His senses faild, his armes were folded straight,
And now he sighes, and then his heart is stung;
Againe he speakes gainst fancies fond deceit,
And teares his tresses with his fingers faire,
And rents his roabs, halfe mad with deepe dispaire.

LXXI

The piteous Nimphes that viewd his heavie plight,
And heard the sequell of his bad successe,
Did loose the springs of their remorsefull sight,
And wept so sore to see his scant redresse:
That of their teares there grew a pretie brooke,

Whose Christall cleares the clowdes of pencive looke.

LXXII

Alas woes me, how oft have I bewept
So faire, so yong, so lovely, and so kinde,
And whilst the God upon my bosome slept,
Behelde the scarres of his afflicted minde,
Imprinted in his yvorie brow by care,
That fruitlesse fancie left unto his share.

LXXIII

My wandring lines, bewitch not so my sences:
But gentle Muse direct their course aright,
Delay es in tragicke tales procure offences:
Yeeld me such feeling words, that whilst I wright,
My working lines may fill mine eyes with languish,
And they to note my mones may melt with anguish.

LXXIV

The wofiill Glaucus thus with woes attainted,
The pencive Nimphes agreevd to see his plight,
The flouds and fields with his laments acquainted,
My selfe amazd to see this heavie sight;
On sodaine Thetis with her traine approched,
And gravely thus her amorous sonne reproched:

LXXV

My sonne (said she), immortall have I made thee,
Amidst my watrie realmes who may compare
Or match thy might? Why then should care invade thee,
That art so yong, so lovely, fresh and faire.
Alas fond God, it merits great reproving
In States of worth, to doate on foolish loving.

LXXVI

Come wend with me, and midst thy Fathers bowre
Let us disport and frolicke for a while
In spite of Love: although he powte and lowre,

Good exercise will idle lusts beguile:
Let wanton Scilla coy her where she will,
Live thou my sonne, by reasons levell still.

LXXVII

Thus said the Goddesse: and although her words
Gave signes of counsaile, pompe and majestie:
Yet nathelesse her piteous eye affoords
Some pretie witnesse to the standers by,
That in her thoughts (for all her outward show)
She mournd to see her Sonne amated so.

LXXVIII

But (welladay) her words have little force;
The hapless lover worne with working woe,
Upon the ground lay pale as any corse,
And were not teares which from his eyes did flowe,
And sighes that witnesse he enjoyd his breath,
They might have thought him Citizen of death.

LXXIX

Which spectacle of care made Thetis bow,
And call on Glaucus, and command her Sonne
To yeelde her right: and hir advice allow,
But (woe) the man whome fancie had undone
Nill marke her rules: nor words, nor weeping teares
Can fasten counsaile in the lovers eares.

LXXX

The Queene of Sea, with all hir Nimphes assured
That no perswasion might releeve his care:
Kneeling adowne, their faltring tongues enured
To tempt faire Venus by their vowed praier:
The course whereof as I could beare in minde
With sorrowing sobbes they uttered in this kinde:

LXXXI

Borne of the Sea, thou Paphian Queene of love,
Mistris of sweete conspiring harmonie:

Lady of Cipris, for whose sweete behove
The Shepeheards praise the youth of Thessalie:
Daughter of Jove and Sister to the Sonne,
Assist poore Glaucus late by love undone.

LXXXII

So maist thou baine thee in th' Arcadian brookes,
And play with Vulcans rivall when thou list,
And calme his jealous anger by thy lookes,
And knit thy temples with a roseat twist
If thou thy selfe and thine almightie Sonne,
Assist poore Glaucus late by love undone.

LXXXIII

May earth still praise thee for her kinde increase:
And beasts adore thee for their fruitfull wombes,
And fowles with noates thy praises never cease,
And Bees admire thee for their honnie combes:
So thou thy selfe and thine almightie Sonne,
Assist poore Glaucus late by love undone.

LXXXIV

No sooner from her reverent lips were past
Those latter lines; but mounting in the East,
Faire Venus in her ivorie coatch did hast,
And toward those pencive dames, her course addrest;
Her doves so plied their waving wings with flight,
That straight the sacred Goddesse came in sight.

LXXXV

Upon her head she bare that gorgeous Crowne,
Wherein the poore Amyntas is a starre;
Her lovely lockes her bosome hang adowne,
(Those netts that first insnar'd the God of warre:)
Delicious lovely shine her prettie eies,
And one her cheekes carnatioon cloudes arise,

LXXXVI

The stately roab she ware upon her back

Was lillie white, wherein with cullored silke,
Her Nimphes had blaz'd the yong Adonis wrack,
And Laedas rape by Swan as white as milke,
And on her lap her lovely Sonne was plaste,
Whose beautie all his mothers pompe defaste.

LXXXVII

A wreath of roses hem'd his Temples in,
His tresse was curlde and cleere as beaten gold;
Haught were his lookes, and lovely was his skin,
Each part as pure as Heavens eternall mold,
And on his eies a milkewhite wreath was spred,
Which longst his backe, with prettie pleits did shed.

LXXXIII

Two daintie wings of partie coulored plumes
Adorne his shoulders dallying with the winde;
His left hand weelds a Torch, that ever fumes:
And in his right, his bowe that fancies bind,
And on his back his Quiver hangs well stored
With sundrie shaftes, that sundrie hearts have gored.

LXXXIX

The Deities ariv'd in place desired;
Faire Venus her to Thetis first bespake,
Princesse of Sea (quoth she), as you required
From Ceston with my Sonne my course I take:
Frollick faire Goddesse, Nimphs forsake your plaining,
My Sonne hath power and favour yet remaining.

XC

With that the reverend powres each other kissed,
And Cupid smil'd upon the Nimphes for pleasure:
So naught but Glaucus solace there was missed,
Which to effect the Nimphes withouten measure
Intreate the God, who at the last drewe nie
The place, where Glaucus full of care did lie,

XCI

And from his bowe a furious dart hee sent
Into that wound which he had made before:
That like Achilles sworde became the teint
To cure the wound that it had carv'd before:
And sodeinly the Sea-god started up:
Revivde, relievd, and free from Fancies cup.

XCII

No more of love, no more of hate he spoke,
No more he forst the sighes from out his breast:
His sodaine joye his pleasing smiles provoke,
And all aloft he shakes his bushie creast,
Greeting the Gods and Goddesses beside,
And everie Nimph upon that happie tide.

XCIII

Cupid and he together hand in hand
Approach the place of this renowned traine:
Ladies (said he), releast from amorous band,
Receive my prisoner to your grace againe.
Glaucus gave thankes, when Thetis glad with blisse
Embrast his neck, and his kind cheekes did kisse

XCIV

To see the Nimphes in flockes about him play,
How Nais kempt his head, and washt his browes:
How Thetis checkt him with his welladay,
How Clore told him of his amorous vowes,
How Venus praised him for his faithfull love,
Within my heart a sodein joy did move.

XCV

Whilst in this glee this holy troope delight,
Along the streame a farre faire Scilla floated,
And coilie vaunst hir creast in open sight:
Whose beauties all the tides with wonder noated,
Fore whom Palemon and the Tritons danced
Whilst she hir limmes upon the tide advanced.

XCVI

Whose swift approach made all the Godheads wonder
Glaucus gan smile to see his lovelie foe,
Rage almost rent poore Thetis heart asonder:
Was never happie troope confused so
As were these deities and daintie dames,
When they beheld the cause of Glaucus blames.

XCVII

Venus commends the carriage of her eye,
Nais upbraides the dimple in her chinne,
Cupid desires to touch the wantons thie,
Clore she sweares that everie eie dooth sinne
That likes a Nimph that so contemneth love,
As no attempts her lawles heart may move.

XCVIII

Thetis impatient of her wrong sustained,
With envious teares her roseat cheekes afflicted;
And thus of Scillas former pride complained;
Cupid (said she), see her that hath inflicted
The deadlie wound that harmde my lovelie sonne,
From whome the offspring of my care begonne.

XCIX

Oh if there dwell within thy brest, my boy
Or grace, or pittie, or remorse (said she),
Now bend thy bowe, abate yon wantons joy,
And let these Nimphes thy rightfull justice see.
The God soone won, gan shoote, and cleft her heart
With such a shaft as causd her endles smart.

C

The tender Nimph attainted unawares,
Fares like the Libian Lionesse that flies
The Hunters Launce that wounds her in his snares;
Now gins shee love, and straight on Glaucus cries;
Whilst on the shore the goddesses rejoyce,

And all the Nimphes afflict the ayre with noyse.

CI

To shoare she flitts, and swift as Affrick wind
Her footing glides upon the yeelding grasse,
And wounded by affect recure to finde
She sodainely with sighes approcht the place
Where Glaucus sat, and wearie with her harmes
Gan claspe the Sea-god in her amorous armes.

CII

Glaucus my love (quoth she), looke on thy lover,
Smile gentle Glaucus on the Nimph that likes thee;
But starke as stone sat he, and list not prove her:
(Ah silly Nimph the selfesame God that strikes thee
With fancies darte, and hath thy freedom slaine)
Wounds Glaucus with the arrowe of disdaine.

CIII

Oh kisse no more kind Nimph, he likes no kindnes,
Love sleepes in him, to flame within thy brest;
Cleer'd are his eies, where thine are clad with blindnes;
Free'd be his thoughts, where thine must taste unrest:
Yet nill she leave, for never love will leave her,
But fruiteles hopes and fatall happes deceave her.

CIV

Lord how her lippes doo dwell upon his cheekes;
And how she lookes for babies in his eies:
And how she sighes, and sweares shee loves and leekes,
And how she vowes, and he her vowes envies:
Trust me the envious Nimphes in looking on,
Were forst with teares for to assist her mone.

CV

How oft with blushes would she plead for grace,
How oft with whisperings would she tempt his eares:
How oft with Christall did she wet his face:

How oft she wipte them with her Amber heares:
So oft me thought, I oft in heart desired
To see the end whereto disdaine aspired.

CVI

Palemon with the Tritons roare for griefe,
To see the Mistris of their joyes amated:
But Glaucus scornes the Nimph, that waites reliefe:
And more she loves, the more the Sea-god hated,
Such change, such chance, such sutes, such storms beleeveme
Poore silly wretch did hartely agreeve me.

CVII

As when the fatall bird of Augurie
Seeing a stormie dismall cloude arise
Within the South, foretells with piteous crie
The weeping tempest, that on sudden hies:
So she poore soule, in view of his disdaine
Began to descant on her future paine.

CVIII

And fixing eye upon the fatall ground,
Whole hoasts of flouds drew deaw from out her eyes;
And when through inward griefe the lasse did sound,
The softned grasse like billowes did arise
To woe her brests, and wed her limmes so daintie,
Whom wretched love had made so weake and faintie.

CIX

(Ayes me), me thinks I see her Thetis fingers
Renting her locks as she were woe begon her;
And now her lippes upon his lipping lingers:
Oh lingring paine, where love nill list to mone her:
Rue me that writes, for why her ruth deserves it:
Hope needs must faile, where sorrow scarce preserves it.

CX

To make long tale were tedious to the wofull,

Wofull that read what wofull shee approoved:
In briefe her heart with deepe dispaire was full,
As since she might not win her sweete beloved.
With hideous cries like winde borne backe she fled
Unto the Sea, and to ward Sicillia sped.

CXI

Sweete Zephirus upon that fatall howre
In haples tide midst watrie world was walking;
Whose milder sighes, alas, had little power
To whisper peace amongst the Godheads talking:
Who all in one conclude for to pursue,
The haples Nimph, to see what would ensue.

CXII

Venus her selfe and her faire Sonne gan hie
Within their ivorie Coach drawne forth by doves
After this haples Nimph, their power to trie:
The Nimphes in hope to see their vowed loves,
Gan cut the watrie boosom of the tide,
As in Cayster Phoebus birds doe glide.

CXIII

Thetis in pompe upon a Tritons back
Did poast her straight, attended by her traine;
But Glaucus free from love by lovers wrack,
Seeing me pencive where I did remaine,
Upon a Dolphin horst me (as he was)
Thus on the Ocean hand in hand we passe.

CXIV

Our talke midway was nought but still of wonder,
Of change, of chaunce, of sorrow, and her ending;
I wept for want: he said, time bringes men under,
And secret want can finde but small befrending.
And as he said, in that before I tried it,
I blamde my wit forewarnd, yet never spied it.

CXV

What neede I talke the order of my way,
Discourse was steeresman while my barke did saile,
My ship conceit, and fancie was my bay:
(If these faile me, then faint my Muse and faile,)
Hast brought us where the haples Nimph sojourned,
Beating the weeping waves that for her mourned.

CXVI

He that hath seene the Northren blastes dispoile
The pompe of Prime, and with a whistling breath
Blast and dispearse the beauties of the soile;
May thinke upon her paines more worse than death.
Alas poore Lasse, the Ecchoes in the rockes
Of Sicilie, her piteous plaining mockes.

CXVII

Eccho her selfe, when Scilla cried out O love!
With piteous voice from out her hollow den,
Returnd these words, these words of sorrow, (no love)
No love (quoth she), then fie on traiterous men,
Then fie on hope: then fie on hope (quoth Eccho)
To everie word the Nimph did answere so.

CXVIII

For every sigh, the Rockes returnes a sigh;
For everie teare, their fountaines yeelds a drop;
Till we at last the place approached nigh,
And heard the Nimph that fed on sorrowes sop
Make woods, and waves, and rockes, and hills admire
The wonderous force of her untam'd desire.

CXIX

Glaucus (quoth she) is faire: whilst Eccho sings
Glaucus is faire: but yet he hateth Scilla
The wretch reportes: and then her armes she wrings
Whilst Eccho tells her this, he hateth Scilla,
No hope (quoth she): no hope (quoth Eccho) then.
Then fie on men: when she said, fie on men.

CXX

Furie and Rage, Wan-hope, Dispaire, and Woe
From Ditis den by Ate sent, drewe nie:
Furie was red, with rage his eyes did gloe,
Whole flakes of fire from foorth his mouth did flie,
His hands and armes ibath'd in blood of those
Whome fortune, sinne, or fate made Countries foes.

CXXI

Rage, wan and pale upon a Tiger sat,
Knawing upon the bones of mangled men;
Naught can he view, but he repinde thereat:
His lockes were Snakes bred foorth in Stigian den,
Next whom, Dispaire that deepe disdained elf
Delightlesse livde, still stabbing of her self.

CXXII

Woe all in blacke, within her hands did beare
The fatall torches of a Funerall,
Her Cheekes were wet, dispearsed was hir heare,
Her voice was shrill (yet loathsome therewith all):
Wan-hope (poore soule) on broken Ancker sitts,
Wringing his armes as robbed of his witts.

CXXIII

These five at once the sorrowing Nimph assaile,
And captive lead her bound into the rocks.
Where howling still she strives for to prevaile,
With no availe yet strives she: for hir locks
Are chang'd with wonder into hideous sands,
And hard as flint become her snow-white hands.

CXXIV

The waters howle with fatall tunes about her,
The aire dooth scoule when as she turnes within them,
The winds and waves with puffes and billowes skout her;
Waves storme, aire scoules, both wind & waves begin them
To make the place this mournful Nimph doth weepe in,

A haples haunt whereas no Nimph may keepe in.

CXXV

The Sea-man wandring by that famous Isle,
Shuns all with feare, dispairing Scillaes bowre;
Nimphes, Sea-gods, Syrens when they list to smile
Forsake the haunt of S cilia in that stowre:
Ah Nimphes thought I, if everie coy one felt
The like misshappes, their flintie hearts would melt.

CXXVI

Thetis rejoyst to see her foe deprest,
Glaucus was glad, since Scilla was enthrald;
The Nimphs gan smile, to boast their Glaucus rest:
Venus and Cupid in their throanes enstald,
At Thetis beck to Neptunes bowre repaire,
Whereas they feast amidst his pallace faire.

CXXVII

Of pure immortall Nectar is their drinke,
And sweete Ambrosia daintie doo repast them,
The Tritons sing, Palemon smiles to thinke
Upon the chance, and all the Nimphs doo hast them
To trick up mossie garlands where they woon,
For lovely Venus and her conquering Sonne.

CXXVIII

From foorth the fountaines of his mothers store,
Glaucus let flie a daintie Christall baine
That washt the Nimphs with labour tir'd before:
Cupid hee trips among this lovely traine,
Alonely I apart did write this storie
With many a sigh and heart full sad and sorie.

CXXIX

Glaucus when all the Goddesses tooke rest,
Mounted upon a Dolphin full of glee:
Conveide me friendly from this honored feast,

And by the way, such Sonnets song to me,
That all the Dolphins neighbouring of his glide
Daunst with delight, his reverend course beside.

CXXX

At last he left me, where at first he found me,
Willing me let the world and ladies knowe
Of Scillas pride, and then by oath he bound me
To write no more, of that whence shame dooth grow:
Or tie my pen to Pennie-knaves delight,
But live with fame, and so for fame to wright.

L'envoy

Ladies he left me, trust me I missay not.
But so he left me as he wild me tell you:
That Nimphs must yeeld, when faithfull lovers straie not,
Least through contempt, almightie love compell you
With Scilla in the rockes to make your biding
A cursed plague, for womens proud back-sliding.

The Career of Thomas Lodge

One of the first to take up the new fashion of the sonnet-cycle, was Thomas Lodge, whose "Phillis" was published in 1595. Lodge had a wide acquaintance among the authors of his time, and was in the thick of the literary activity in the last two decades of the sixteenth century. In his own time he may have appeared as a literary dilettante, who tried his hand at several forms of writing, and being outshone by the more excellent in each field, gave up the attempt and turned to the practice of medicine. This profession engaged him for the last twenty-five years of his life, until his death in 1625 at the advanced age of sixty-seven or eight. During all these years the gay young "university wit" of earlier days was probably forgotten in the venerable and successful physician. It was as "old Doctor Lodge" that he was satirised in a Cambridge student's Common-place Book in 1611. Heywood mentions him in 1609 among the six most famous physicians in England, and in the Return from Parnassus, a play acted in 1602, he is described as "turning over Galen every day."

Yet no one had been in the last twenty years the sixteenth century more responsive than Lodge to the shifting moods of that excitable period. Lodge was the son of a Lord Mayor of London, and was a contemporary at Oxford with Sidney, Gosson, Chapman, Lyly, Peele and Watson. His life included a round of varied experiences. A student at Lincoln's Inn, a young aspirant for literary honours, friends with Greene, Rich, Daniel, Drayton, Lyly and Watson, a taster of the sorrows that many of the University wits endured when usurers got their hands upon them, for a time perhaps a soldier, certainly a sailor following the fortunes of Captain Clarke to Terceras and the Canaries, and of Cavendish to Brazil and the Straits of Magellan, in London again making plays with Greene, off to Avignon to take his degree in medicine, back again to be incorporated an M.D. at Oxford and to practise in London, adopting secretly the Roman Catholic faith, and sometimes hiding on the continent as a recusant from persecution at home, imprisoned perhaps once for debt, and entertaining a concourse of patients of his own religion till his death in 1625:—the life of Lodge thus presents a view of the ups and downs possible in that picturesque age.

The wide variety of his literary ventures reflects the interests of his life. Some controversial papers, some unsuccessful plays, two dull historical sketches in prose, some satirical and moralising works in prose and in verse, two romantic tales in verse and three in prose, a number of eclogues, metrical epistles and lyrics, some ponderous translations from Latin and French, and two medical treatises; these widely differing kinds of writing are the products of Lodge's industry and genius. All, however, have but an antiquarian interest save two; the prose romance called Rosalynde, Euphues' Golden Legacy, could not be spared since Shakespeare borrowed its charming plot for As You Like It; and Phillis, bound up with a sheaf of his lyrics gathered from the pages of his stories and from the miscellanies of the time, should be treasured for its own sake and should keep Lodge's memory green for lovers of pure poetry.

Lodge's lyric genius was a clear, if slender, rill. His faults are the more unpardonable since they spring from sheer carelessness and a lack of appreciation of the sacred responsibility of creative power. He took up the literary fashion of the month and tried his hand at it; that done, he was ready for the next mode. He did not wait to perfect his work or to compare result with result; therefore he probably never found himself, probably never realised that after three centuries he would be esteemed, not for the ponderous tomes of his translation of Josephus, not for all the catalogues of his satirical and religious and scientific writings, but for mere lyrics like the "Heigh ho, fair Rosaline," and "Love in my bosom like a bee," heedlessly imbedded in the heart of a prose romance.

Lodge was one of the earliest to follow the example of Sidney in linking a sequence of sonnets together into a sonnet-cycle. The Astrophel and Stella was published in 1591, though it had doubtless before this been handed about, as was the Elizabethan fashion, in manuscript. Early in 1591 also when Daniel was probably abroad, twenty-seven of the fifty-seven sonnets that a year later formed the sonnet-cycle Delia were published in his absence. Now in August of 1591 Lodge set sail with Cavendish on that long voyage to Brazil and the Straits of Magellan from which he did not return till early in ninety-three, and it was during his absence that Daniel's and Constable's sonnet-cycles came out. It is possible that Lodge saw Daniel's series, as he doubtless did Sidney's, in manuscript before he left England, but the Induction to Phillis, which carries a message to Delia's "sweet prophet," was almost certainly written later, and in the absence of further proof it seems no more than fair to allow Lodge to share with Daniel and Constable the honour of being the earliest to take the hint Sidney had offered.

On the whole, Lodge's sonnets show a much more cheerful and buoyant temper than Daniel's "wailing verse." The "sad horror, pale grief, prostrate despair" that inform the Delia, are replaced in the Phillis by a spirit of airy toying, a pleasure in the graces of fancy even when they cluster around a feeling of sadness. During Lodge's absence, his friend Robert Green published several pieces for him, and in one of the prefaces promised the public to present on his return "what labours Lodge's sea-studies afford." Phillis was the chief of these sea-studies, and was like Rosalynde "hatcht in the stormes of the ocean and feathered in the surges of many perillous seas." But as far as the imagery of the sonnets is concerned, the pageantry of day and night at sea might have passed before blinded eyes; if it made any impression, it was in the form of ocean-nymphs and Cupid at the helm. The poet was in Arcadia, Phillis was a shepherdess, and the conventional imageries of the pastoral valley were the environment. "May it please you," he says in dedicating the book to the Countess of Shrewsbury, "to looke and like of homlie

Phillis in her Country caroling, and to countenance her poore and affectionate sheapheard." The Countess of Shrewsbury he chooses for the "Sovereign and she-Mæcenas" of his toil, and promises her "as much in affection as any other can performe in perfection;" but the name of Phillis is no cover for the personality of a grand lady, and therefore no puzzling questions disturb the pleasure of the reader as the gentle modulations, the insidious alliterations, and the musical cadences of his double rhymes fall upon the ear.

Yet for this name or ideal, or whatever Phillis represented in the poet's thought, he has poured forth a passion that has an air of sincerity, an artless freshness, a flute-like clearness of tone, as rare as delightful. It is the very voice of the oaten pipe itself, thin, clear, and pure. The touches of seriousness are impossible, to mistake. When the poet avows his faith in Phillis' constancy, after giving the usual catalogue of her beauties, he says:

"At thy fair hands who wonders not at all
Wonder itself through ignorance embases;
Yet not the less though wondrous gifts you call these
My faith is far more wonderful than all these."

When Phillis persists in her disdain, he cries out impulsively:

"Burst, burst, poor heart, thou hast no longer hope!"

Even when re-moulding the familiar pastoral conceits, he makes the fancies his own and gives to them a unique touch and spirit. Mere conventions he rates at their proper value. His pen shall not "riot in pompous style." He claims a brighter aspect for his poetical devotion than his fellow-sonneteers manifest:

"No stars her; eyes....
.... but beams that clear the sight
Of him that seeks the true philosophy."

In spite of its defects, the lax structure of the sonnet-form, the obscurities and needless blurring, and the disappointing inequalities, Phillis takes a high place among the sonnet-cycles, and must ever be dear to lovers of quiet, melodious verse, who have made themselves at home in the golden world of the pastoral poets and mislike not the country-carolling heard therein.

The Published Works of Thomas Lodge in Chronological Order

c1580 Defence of Plays
1584 An Alarum Against Usurers
1589 Scillaes Metamorphysis
1590 Rosalynde
1591 Robert, Second Duke of Normandy
1591 Catharos
1592 Euphues Shadow
1593 Phillis

1593 William Longbeard
1594 The Wounds of Civill War
1594 A Looking Glass for London (in collaboration with Robert Greene)
1595 A Fig for Momus
1596 The Divel Conjured
1596 A Margarite of America
1596 Wits Miserie
1596 Prosopopeia
1602 Paradoxes
1602 Works of Josephus
1603 A Treatise of the Plague
1614 The Workes of Seneca
1625 A Learned Summary of Du Bartas